CANADA THROUGH THE DECADES
THE 1930s

Douglas and Patricia Baldwin

Weigl

CALGARY
www.weigl.com

Published by Weigl Educational Publishers Limited
6325 – 10 Street SE
Calgary, Alberta, Canada
T2H 2Z9
Web site: http://www.weigl.com

Canadian Cataloguing in Publication Data

Baldwin, Douglas, 1944–
 The 1930s

 (Canada through the decades)
 Includes bibliographical references and index.
 ISBN 1-896990-64-9

 1. Canada—History—1918–1939—Juvenile literature.* 2. Canada—History—1939–1945—Juvenile literature.* I. Baldwin, Patricia, 1946– II. Title. III. Series.
FC580.B35 1999   j791.062'3   C99-911107-8

Printed and bound in Canada
1 2 3 4 5 6 7 8 9 0   04 03 02 01 00

Editor
Rennay Craats
Design
Warren Clark
Copy Editor
Meaghan Craven
Layout
Chantelle Sales

Photograph Credits

Every reasonable effort has been made to trace ownership and to obtain permission to reprint copyright material. The publishers would be pleased to have any errors or omissions brought to their attention so that they may be corrected in subsequent printings

Archive Photos: pages 11B, 13T-L, 13B-L, 13T-R, 18T, 24T-L, 25B, 27T, 38T, 39T; Canada Sports Hall of Fame: pages 28T, 30B, 34T; Canadian Broadcasting Corporation: page 11T; Canadian Jewish Congress: pages 21B, 36B; Corbis/Bettman Images: pages 13B-R, 14, 15T, 17, 18B, 19T, 34B, 38B, 39B, 40T; Corel Corporation: page 32; Glenbow Archives: pages 8, 9B, 31T, 32L, 33B, 35T, 35B, 36T, 37, 41, 43T; Hockey Hall of Fame: pages 29 30T, 31, 42; Maclean's Magazine: page 24T-R; Manitoba Sports Hall of Fame: page 28B; National Archives of Canada: pages 10, 12T, 15M, 16, 19M, 19B, 20, 22T, 23, 25T, 26, 27B, 35L, 40M, 43B; National Gallery of Canada, Ottawa, "Petroushka" by Paraskeva Clark: page 12B; Provincial Archives of Alberta: page 21, 33T; Provincial Archives of Manitoba: page 22B; Public Archives of Nova Scotia: page 9B; Reader's Digest: page 24B.

CANADA THE 1930s Contents

Economy 32

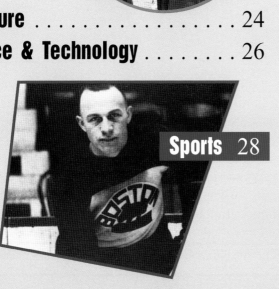

Music 38

Introduction

Salted Cod Aid

Canada's American Sweetheart

Invasion Sparks World War

The Great Depression

Norman Bethune, Chinese Hero

Abdication of King Edward VIII

Work Camps

Winnipeg Wins Cup

On-To-Ottawa Trek

Epilepsy Treatment Discovered

The Dirty Thirties, The Bitter Thirties, The Hungry Thirties, The Depression Years, The Nasty Thirties, The Ten Lost Years. When people think of the 1930s they often imagine dust storms so thick that it was difficult to see across the street. They remember years with almost no rain, long lines of unemployed people looking for jobs, and starving families waiting for food at soup kitchens.

To save on money, children went without socks, shoes and underwear. Young, unmarried men became "knights of the road." They left home, climbed aboard boxcars and travelled around the country looking for work. Desperate men and women went on strike for better wages and working conditions. When nothing seemed to work, people joined radical political parties that promised to help the poor and unemployed.

The Depression began with the stock market crash in 1929 and did not really end until the

Dionne Quints Capture Hearts

S.S. St. Louis Turned Away

Anti-Semitism in Canada

The Hindenburg Mystery

Riot at Christie Pits

Rotten Potatoes, Rotten Tomatoes

Moose River Mine Disaster

Boxing offers Escape

Amelia Earhart Disappears

beginning of World War II in 1939. In between these years, company presidents went broke, the average Canadian's income was cut in half, and about one-third of the country's people were unemployed.

But there were also some good times. Canadians helped each other. They told jokes, went to the movies, and listened to "Hockey Night in Canada" on the radio. They followed the lives of the Dionne quintuplets. They debated whether hockey was becoming too violent.

Canada Through the Decades: The 1930s is a journey through the Dirty Thirties. The stories in these pages cover many important events and people, but only briefly. If you want to find out more information about these stories, visit your library. It has old newspapers and magazines that can offer more information about the 1930s. Encyclopedias, history books, and the Internet are also useful tools for learning about this fascinating decade.

Time Line

1930

Canada goes conservative. **R.B. Bennett** and his Conservative party win the federal election. Turn to page 20 to find out more about this skilled politician.

1931

Starting in 1931, the dust blows and blows across Canada. With the **dust comes drought and Depression**. Find out more on page 8.

1931

A brilliant scientist pushes ahead with his experiments on the brain. Find out what **Wilder Penfield learns about the brain**, and how he uses the information to save lives on page 26.

1932

Amelia Earhart flies high. She becomes the first woman to fly solo across the Atlantic Ocean. Turn to page 19 to learn about her accomplishments and her disappearance.

1932

Marjorie Kirkham paves the way for female golfers. Find out how she challenges Canadians' views of women in sports on page 30.

1932

Hard times in Canada lead to new political parties in the 1930s. The **Co-operative Commonwealth Federation (CCF) is founded**. Find out what the party believes in on page 20.

1932

The Canadian government tries to **put people to work**. The plan does not work out very well. Turn to page 23 to find out why.

1932

Canada says goodbye to its favourite screen star. **Mary Pickford** makes her last movie in 1932. To learn more about this entertainment legend, turn to page 12.

1933

Herbert McCool is taking it easy in 1933. And it makes him a fortune! Find out more about the inventor of **Easy-Off Oven Cleaner** on page 26.

1933

A Canadian actress tames King Kong. For more information about movie actress **Fay Wray**, turn to page 13.

1933

Saturday nights will never be the same. **Hockey Night in Canada** storms onto the radio in 1933. Find out more on page 11.

1933

A baseball game leads to violence in 1933. Racist comments cause **a riot**. Turn to page 23 to find out what started the ruckus.

1933

Adolf Hitler becomes leader of Germany. Find out about his policies and his rise to power on page 16.

1934

"The Vancouver Irishman" swings his way to the top. Page 28 has details about this welterweight champion.

1934

The Dionne family have a baby, and then another, and then three more before they are through! Find out more about the **famous quintuplets** on page 40.

1935

Canadians are **tired of being unemployed**, and they want to do something about it. So, they hop a train to Ottawa. Page 21 tells you how this could help matters.

1935

Winnipeg takes home the championship. The city goes wild for its conquering heroes. Find out what they won on page 28.

1936

The roof comes tumbling down in the **Moose River Mine**. And people across the country know about it. Find out how on page 9.

1936

Spain is in turmoil in 1936. The military army rebelled against the democratic government. Find out how the conflict was resolved on page 19.

1936

Charles Vance Millar's **Stork Derby** comes to an end. Women compete for big money and try to have more babies than anyone else. Find out how this contest came about on page 15.

1936

King Edward VIII is in love and will do anything for his sweetheart. The British monarch makes an enormous sacrifice for love. Find out what he does on page 19.

1937

Canadian writers are recognized with a new award. Find out more about the **Governor General's Award** on page 25.

1937

The **Hindenburg** explodes, and no one knows why. Find out more about the German airship that mysteriously blows up on page 18.

1937

There are nearly 300 **strikes** this year. Employees at General Motors take to the streets, and get some of what they asked for. Find out why on page 33.

1938

Russia lives in fear of its leader. Learn about **Stalin's reign of terror** on page 17.

1938

He is faster than a speeding bullet, and he is a Canadian creation. For details about the arrival of **Superman,** North America's favourite superhero, turn to page 24.

1938

Canadian hockey hero **Eddie Shore** says "no" to a new contract. The owners have no choice but to meet his demands. Find out why they could not just let the player sit the bench on page 29.

1939

Hitler's troops march into Poland, setting **World War II** in motion. Find out more on page 17.

1939

A Canadian hero dies in China. **Norman Bethune** has an impact on thousands of lives around the world. Find out how on page 27.

1939

Canada gives Hollywood a run for its documentary money. **The National Film Board** is founded in 1939. Find out why this organization is important on page 11.

The Dustbowl

There was almost no rainfall on the prairies during much of the 1930s. After several years of **drought**, the topsoil turned into dust. When the wind picked up, it created dust storms. Sometimes the dust was so thick that it was impossible to see across the street. Dust got into everything. It coated people's faces and made eyes bloodshot. In some regions, the dust was so deep that fences disappeared from sight.

The drought was devastating, but many farmers kept their senses of humour. Some told stories of cows wearing sunglasses to protect their eyes during dust storms, and of children being frightened of a

███ Dust clouds literally created walls of dust that sent people running for shelter.

rain shower because they had never seen one before. Some people joked that if they threw a gopher in the air during a dust storm, it would dig a hole before it hit the ground.

One day, a farmer went to a bank to ask for a loan on his farm. The banker said, "I want to see your land before I give you the money." A gust of wind rattled the windows of the bank, and the farmer said, "Well, open up your window, 'cuz here she comes."

GRASSHOPPERS!

███ What the dust storms missed, grasshoppers destroyed. Grasshoppers were so thick on the prairies that some roads became too slippery to walk on. People told stories of grasshoppers covering railroads and stopping trains. Sometimes, Mother Nature was kind. One western farmer told about a flock of gulls who ate every one of the grasshoppers on the farmer's land one day.

Letters to Ottawa

"...I am trying to get a start without any money and five children, all small. Have been trying to send three to school and live on $10 a month relief for everything, medicine, meat, flour, butter, scribblers. Haven't had any milk for three months. ...Am worried on account of the children as we never have any vegetables except potatoes and almost no fruit and baby hasn't any shoes."

Letter to the prime minister from a Burton, Alberta, woman

Salted Cod Aid

To help western Canadian farmers suffering from the Depression, Maritimers sent boxcar loads of canned goods, vegetables, squash, pumpkins, apples, and salted cod. This act of generosity, declared one westerner, "was one of the most inspirational gestures in Canadian history." Such acts helped bring the country together. The dried salted fish, however, was a puzzle to many western farmers. "We soaked it in water, or milk, or any other way we could think of and it still came out salty, dry and tasteless," remembered one farmer. Some people used the salted cod to shingle their outhouses.

Moose River Mine Disaster

On April 12, 1936, three men entered the mine they had bought near Moose River, Nova Scotia. The roof of the mine collapsed, and they were trapped. Rescue operations began almost immediately, and newspaper reporters flocked to the scene.

The Canadian Broadcasting Corporation (CBC) sent Frank Willis to the scene. CBC radio had started in 1932 and broadcast only six hours a day. Unlike newspaper reporters, Willis needed a telephone. But there was only one phone in the village, and thirteen people shared the party line. Fortunately, a mine official cleared the phone line and allowed Willis to use it for five minutes every half hour.

This was the first time such a disaster had been covered live. About 50 million people listened to Willis' hourly broadcasts, which continued night and day for fifty-six hours. Some women phoned their husbands at work to

Frank Willis became famous in Moose River. He later moved on to become a well-respected radio producer.

give regular updates. Other people sat by their radios all day and night waiting to hear what would happen. Finally, the rescuers reached the men. Two were still alive. Willis was so tired by this time that he could hardly speak. He became a celebrity and live radio news had won fans across Canada.

GOPHERS

Gophers overran the prairies. Their numbers multiplied so quickly that the government offered money for each one killed. For many people, this was the only way to earn spending money. In the first years of the 1930s, more than two million gophers were killed per year.

Radio Shows

Like television today, radio was the focus of many homes. It provided drama, sports, music, news, and comedy. Virtually all radio shows were live. This made for many embarrassing slips. For example, an announcer once called British politician Stafford Cripps "Stifford Crapps." Despite these slip-ups, radio was very popular. Perhaps the most loved Canadian radio show was "The Happy Gang," which played music and told corny jokes. Listeners often mailed in their own corny jokes.

Radio dramas were also popular. Squeaking floors, devilish laughs, screams, and good plots kept listeners on the edge of their seats. H.G. Wells's *War of the Worlds* was so realistic that many people actually believed that Earth was being invaded from outer space.

This was the era of radio comedy. When Jack Benny began broadcasting in 1932, he found it difficult telling jokes into the speaker, so he created the first studio audience.

Benny pretended to be very stingy with his money and on every program the other cast members made fun of him for it. In one broadcast, a "robber" approached Benny and demanded "Your money or your life." Then followed the longest pause in radio history. Listeners began to laugh as they got the joke. Finally, Benny said, "All right. I'm thinking about it."

■ Radio personalities Jack Benny (left) and Mary Livingstone were a hit with Canadians, even Prime Minister Mackenzie King.

DAVID MILNE

■ David Milne worked as a book and magazine illustrator before deciding to devote his time to painting. Preferring the peace and solitude of rural life, Milne built a **secluded** cabin at Six Mile Lake, north of Orillia, Ontario. He spent six years painting—for the most part on his own.

He painted everything from landscapes to urban scenes to imaginary subjects. He liked to experiment with different shapes, and viewpoints. Milne called his watercolours "adventures in shape, colour, texture and space." When his son, David Jr., was born, Milne focussed more on creating imaginary scenes in his art.

Milne's paintings did not become popular until late in his life. He was able to continue painting without a real income thanks to the support of several wealthy people. He was disappointed by Canada's feelings toward the arts. He felt that most Canadians were interested only in their belongings, their families, and their pets. He thought that Canadians did not have the time for or interest in art.

Hockey Night in Canada

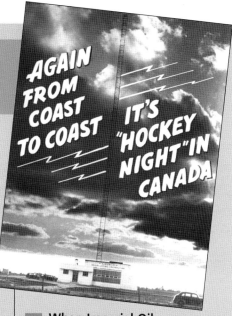

"**H**e shoots! He scores!" In the 1930s, these words were heard in almost every town in Canada. The Leafs games in Mutual Street Arena in Toronto were broadcast locally over radio station CFCA. Beginning on January 1, 1933, listeners from coast to coast could hear Foster Hewitt's play-by-play broadcasts of the Leafs' Saturday night games from Maple Leaf Gardens. This was one of the first Canadian radio programs for a national audience. Soon, Hewitt's vivid descriptions attracted large audiences. By 1934, more than a million fans listened in to Hewitt's famous opening line, "Hello Canada and hockey fans in the United States and Newfoundland." That year, an estimated 72 percent of all Canadian radio sets tuned into his broadcast of the Stanley Cup semi-finals. After the playoffs, 90,000 listeners wrote to thank Foster Hewitt.

When Imperial Oil became the sponsor of Hockey Night in Canada, it wanted to promote its new brand of gasoline, "Three Stars." This is the origin of the three stars at the end of every hockey game.

By the end of the decade, Hockey Night in Canada's audience had increased to more than 2 million listeners, and Hewitt was receiving letters from places as distant as lighthouses on the east coast, trawlers off the North Atlantic fishing banks, and Hudson's Bay trading posts in the North.

WORLD FOCUS

OSCAR-WINNING CHILD STAR

In 1935, Shirley Temple became the youngest person ever to win an Academy Award. The seven-year-old superstar began acting at three years old, and starred in hit movies including Bright Eyes, *in which she sang "On the Good Ship Lollipop." Movies such as* Little Miss Marker, *and* Stand Up and Cheer *helped make the youngster a household name. And these were only a few of the more than twenty movies she starred in during the 1930s alone. Shirley Temple captured North America's heart, and even had a non-alcoholic drink named after her.*

National Film Board Created

In 1939, the federal government passed a law that created a National Film Commission. It was soon known as the National Film Board (NFB). This agency worked with the Government Motion Picture Bureau to make films that helped Canadians throughout Canada understand each other. The National Film Board also coordinated the film needs of government departments.

When Canada entered World War II, the Film Board began producing **propaganda** films to promote the war effort. Canada became well known for war films during this time.

In 1939, John Grierson became the first Government Film Commissioner. He was a well-respected documentary filmmaker, and the NFB became famous for their documentaries. "Documentary" was a term that Grierson created in 1926. He negotiated an agreement that allowed the distribution of National Film Board productions in the United States. Famous Players of Canada, which had 800 theatres across the country, showed the films within Canada.

America's Canadian Sweetheart

Mary Pickford was born in Toronto in 1892. At that time her name was Gladys Marie Smith. Her parents were both actors and Smith followed in their footsteps. Called "Baby Gladys Smith," she began her acting career at the age of six. In 1907, she changed her name to Mary Pickford.

Pickford acted all the time. She did not have time to go to school so she taught herself to read. All of her hard work paid off. In 1908, at the age of sixteen, Pickford starred in her first film. She was now being called "the girl with the golden hair." By 1909, Pickford was in high demand. She made fifty-one films, and by the time she was twenty, she had appeared in 176 movies. In the United States, her nickname was "America's Sweetheart." She was also called "the World's Sweetheart."

Mary Pickford soon reduced her heavy acting load. She turned her attention to writing and producing movies instead

▇ **Mary Pickford started acting when she was five. Her earnings helped support her family.**

of starring in them. More importantly, in 1919, she helped to start United Artists Studio, which was later bought by MGM. Pickford knew what movies would work and what ones would flop. Later, she helped to create the Academy of Motion Picture Arts and Sciences, the organization that awards Oscars to the best motion pictures and performers.

In 1932, Mary made her final film, *Star Night at the Coconut Grove*. It was her 263rd movie.

Mary Pickford died on May 29, 1979. She is still thought of as a film industry legend.

SOCIAL REALISM IN ART

▇ In the 1930s, artists began to view Canada in a different way. The landscapes of art in the 1920s were gone, and **realism** was back. Instead of landscapes celebrating Canada's beauty, painters showed how the Depression affected people. Miller Brittain, for example, painted unemployed dock workers from Saint John, New Brunswick. Carl Schaefer painted watercolours showing agricultural machinery rusting in the fields. Jack Humphrey painted portraits of children in Saint John with sad, pathetic eyes. Paraskeva Clark painted real people and their daily lives. This style of art was called "social realism." It showed life as it was, regardless of whether it was happy or miserable.

FAMOUS MOVIES FROM HOLLYWOOD'S GOLDEN ERA

Animal Crackers (1930)
— Marx Brothers

Dracula (1931) — Bela Lugosi

Frankenstein (1931) — Boris Karloff

Duck Soup (1933) — Marx Brothers

■ "One morning I shot an elephant in my pyjamas. How he got into my pyjamas, I'll never know."
—from *Animal Crackers*

A Night at the Opera (1935) — Marx Brothers

Top Hat (1935) — Fred Astaire and Ginger Rogers

■ Ginger Rogers and Fred Astaire were Hollywood favourites. They made ten movies together.

Modern Times (1936)
— Charlie Chaplin

Snow White (1937) /The Three Little Pigs (1933) — Disney animation

Stagecoach (1939) — John Wayne

The Wizard of Oz (1939)
— Judy Garland

Mounties in the Movies

North Americans loved the image of the mountie. Mounties were used in many movies as a symbol of the honourable Canadian. In 1936, American actor Nelson Eddy played a Canadian Mountie in *Rose Marie*. In the plot, Eddy falls in love with a beautiful singer, played by Jeannette MacDonald. But MacDonald is not who she seems. She is hoping to rescue her brother who has escaped from prison after killing a Mountie. When Eddy discovers her real purpose,

■ The mountie in *Rose Marie* does what is right, but he manages to walk away with the girl, too.

he has to choose between duty and love. Of course, he chooses duty.

Fay Wray Conquers King Kong

Fay Wray was born in Medicine Hat, Alberta, in 1907 and was raised in Los Angeles, California. She began acting in 1923 and met with immediate success when she starred in *The Wedding March* in 1928.

But when people think of Wray, they often think of screaming. Her **shrill** shriek was heard throughout her most famous movie. She starred as the beauty who captured the beast's heart in *King Kong* in 1933. Fay Wray also wrote many plays and stories, as well as the story of her life entitled *On the Other Hand*.

■ Fay Wray's most famous role was opposite a giant ape. She continued to star in movies until 1958.

False Advertising

In the 1930s, there were few laws against false advertising. Since companies were not required to list ingredients on labels, some foods even contained poisonous ingredients. Other companies used false bottoms to make their boxes seem to contain more than they did. Labels that claimed a product was made of a blend of wool and cotton sometimes contained almost no wool. Electric lights advertised as burning for 1,000 hours burned out after 662 hours. "Pure cotton" was often mixed with filler. Brand name labels were sewn on no-brand clothes.

Tired of the false claims, women across the country led a campaign against false advertising. They protested on the streets, **boycotted** stores that charged too much, and picketed companies because of their unfair practices.

Toys All Year

Advertisements targeted children and their mothers. In past years, toy-giving stopped when a child reached his or her teens. Instead of giving children toys only on their birthdays and holidays, mothers were encouraged to buy toys year-round. Toy producers persuaded parents that childhood should last a bit longer through toys.

Shirley Temple Dolls

Dolls resembling child actor Shirley Temple were the "rage." But at around $12, they were too expensive for many families to afford. One department store salesclerk remembered watching the faces of little girls, from 4 to 11 years old, as they looked in the windows at blonde-haired Shirley Temple dolls. Many of the children were starving, but they would stare at the dolls for hours. "They were lucky if they had breakfast that morning, or soup and bread that night, but they came every day to stare at the dolls," she recalled.

■ Young girls dreamed of owning a Shirley Temple doll. The curly-haired beauty remained just a dream for many. Few families in the 1930s could afford to buy the toy.

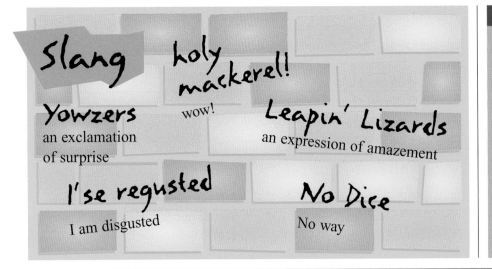

Slang

Yowzers
an exclamation of surprise

holy mackerel!
wow!

Leapin' Lizards
an expression of amazement

I'se regusted
I am disgusted

No Dice
No way

SMALLER FAMILIES

■ How many brothers and sisters does the average person in your class have? In the 1930s, the average number of children per family fell from 3.4 to 2.8. Few people wanted to have children when they were unemployed. Some women nursed longer to save on food.

Get Rich Quick!

Many people were conned out of their money by the idea that they could get rich without much work. Ten-cent chain letters were a very common form of the get-rich-quick scheme. A letter was sent that instructed the receiver to send a dime to each of three addresses on the bottom of the page. The receiver was to then send the letter to three other people and add their own name to the bottom of the list. If the receiver did not follow the instructions, they would have three years of bad luck. The government soon banned the scheme.

Manners

Choose which of the following was considered rude in the 1930s.

- sitting down to dinner before the hostess was seated
- asking for anything at the dinner table, such as vinegar or butter—this would suggest that the host was at fault
- putting an olive stone in your mouth
- putting a fork in your mouth with the prongs turned up
- eating with your mouth open
- using toothpicks in public
- manicuring nails in public
- borrowing money from a woman
- being photographed in evening clothes
- smoking in front of a lady

Answer: All

FADS

- New products:
  - canned soups and baby foods
  - cellophane wrappers for food
  - aluminum, rayon, and Nylon
- Most popular comic:
  - *Amos 'n' Andy*.
- Two favourite sayings from this comic:
  - "Holy Mackerel!" and "I'se regusted" (I am disgusted).

- Popular pastimes:
  - rollerskating
  - Monopoly
  - miniature golf

The Stork Derby

Toronto lawyer Charles Vance Millar died in 1926. His will left a fortune to the Toronto woman who gave birth to the most children in the next 10 years. Many women competed. In the end, five women tied with nine children won. The women each received $165,000. They donated $12,500 to another woman who had been disqualified from the contest.

Charles Millar's sense of humour shone through in other parts of his will. He left shares in a **jockey club** to a minister who was against horse racing and betting. He left ownership of his summer home in Jamaica to three people who strongly disliked each other, but he left nothing for his relatives.

DROPPING THE LEAGUE OF NATIONS

■ The League of Nations was created after World War I. It was supposed to keep peace between countries of the world. It failed.

In 1933, Germany pulled out of the international organization. The League would not change the restrictions placed on Germany's military after World War I, so Germany left. Japan also dropped out of the League of Nations. It had invaded Manchuria, and member nations would not support Japanese control over that country. Italy later withdrew from the League of Nations in 1937 to join forces with Japan and Germany. The countries, called the Axis Powers, started World War II.

The Rise of Hitler

World War I left Germany **bankrupt** and bitter. People blamed the problems on the democratic government that had signed the peace agreement. Adolf Hitler used these feelings to his advantage. He and his Nazi Party presented themselves as the answers to Germany's problems.

Hitler quickly built up party membership. Members wore **swastikas** on their uniforms, gave victory salutes, and marched like robots through the streets. There was finally a sense of belonging that had been lost to many Germans since World War I.

But Nazi support dropped in the 1932 election. The following year,

■ Hitler conquered most of Europe before being defeated in 1945.

President Hindenburg appointed the Nazi leader chancellor. Some officials hoped that this might be a way to control Hitler. It was not. Hitler called a snap election for March, and was voted Germany's leader in 1933.

Dictatorships

■ People hoped dictators could solve their countries' problems.

Hard economic times often led to extreme political situations. When countries do not have a long history of democracy, it is often the first thing to go. This happened in the 1930s in Italy, Germany, and several other European countries. In Latin America, the turn to **dictatorships** also increased.

Growth of Dictatorships in Latin America

Brazil,
G. Vargas, 1930

Dominican Republic,
R. Trujillo, 1930

Guatemala,
J. Ubico, 1930

El Salvador,
M. Martinez, 1932

Honduras,
T. Andino, 1932

Cuba,
F. Batista, 1933

Nicaragua,
A. Somoza Garcia, 1936

THE ENABLING ACT

Hitler passed the Enabling Act soon after the election. This meant that he did not have to answer to anyone for his actions. He focussed his attention on getting rid of Jewish people in Germany. He blamed Jews for World War I and thought they were **inferior**.

Hitler called for a boycott of all Jewish businesses. All non-Jews were told not to do business with Jews. The head of police would not stop people from attacking or robbing Jews. Hitler also enacted laws that would not allow Jews to be teachers, doctors, lawyers, or go to university. By 1935, hatred against Jews was legal, and Jews were not allowed to vote or marry non-Jewish people. Hitler's policies continued to terrorize the Jewish community. Many people feared what would happen with Hitler leading the country.

Invasion Sparks World War II

German troops invaded Poland, setting in motion World War II.

On August 31, 1939, the German army attacked Poland. More than one million German troops marched over the border between the two countries. Adolf Hitler wanted to take back the parts of Poland Germany had lost during World War I. Joseph Stalin, leader of Russia, was also interested in gaining some Polish land. He and Hitler agreed not to fight each other, and turned their attention to taking over Poland—Hitler later broke his word to Stalin.

Britain and France had already promised to help Poland if it was attacked. Germany did not think these countries would put up much of a fight. They guessed wrong. Great Britain and France gave Germany two days to leave Poland or be prepared to fight their armies as well. Germany did not pull out. World War II began.

Stalin's Reign of Terror

Joseph Stalin ruled the Soviet Union with terror from 1929 until 1953.

Joseph Stalin was the most hated man in Moscow. The Russian dictator ruled his country with cruelty and brutality. After coming into power, he had Russian history rewritten. In 1938, he helped write the official history of the Communist party.

In 1935, Stalin started to get rid of people who had supported the former leader, Vladimir Lenin. Stalin's police terrorized or killed citizens. Some people were sent to work camps. Stalin also had anyone who may have been a threat to him killed. He killed chiefs and officers in his army as well as members of his party. His plan was successful. By the time World War II started, there was no one left to oppose Russia's involvement in the fighting.

The Hindenburg Mystery

The Hindenburg was a fancy, hydrogen-filled airship made by the Germans. In 1937, as it was preparing to land in New Jersey, the airship suddenly burst into flames. In a matter of seconds, the ship became a ball of fire. Even now, surviving eye witnesses cannot forget the horrible experience. Thirty-five people died.

What had caused the disaster? Some said it was a bomb planted by Hitler's enemies. Others said the Hindenburg was struck by lightning. Was it a way to get money from insurance claims? What caused the explosion?

Germany, afraid other countries might learn about its technology, would not help the investigation. The mystery was never solved.

The Hindenburg was the last airship used for passenger service.

Italian Aggression

Italy was at war for most of the thirties. When it looked like Italy might attack Ethiopia in 1936, the United States, Great Britain, and France said they would not get involved. Ethiopian Emperor Haile Sellassie thought this was unfair. Ethiopia was an agricultural country without the weapons to defend itself. Italy was a strong country that could give its soldiers modern weapons. Only Germany sold weapons to Ethiopia in an effort to weaken Italy.

When Italy did attack, it bombed Ethiopia with **mustard gas**, a poison used in warfare.

Ethiopia could not defend itself against this terrible weapon. But Ethiopians fought hard. One soldier who operated one of the country's few anti-aircraft guns became injured but refused to leave his post. He later died from an infection in an injured leg. He likely would have survived had he

Italian troops took Ethiopia without much trouble. The rest of the world would not step in to help the outgunned African country.

gone to the hospital. Despite these efforts, on May 9, 1936, the war was over. Italy had won control over Ethiopia.

Amelia Earhart Disappears

Amelia Earhart became a household name in 1932 when she became the first woman, and the second person, to fly solo across the Atlantic Ocean. The flight left from Harbor Grace, Newfoundland, and landed in Londonderry, Ireland.

Three years later, Earhart became the first to fly solo across the Pacific Ocean—from Honolulu to Oakland, California. In 1936, she began to plan for an around-the-world flight at the equator. This would be the longest single flight ever made (50,000 kilometres).

Fred Noonan was Earhart's navigator and sole companion for the trip. They left Miami, Florida, on June 1, 1937, and after stops in South America, Africa, and Southeast Asia,

"You will find the unexpected everywhere you go in life. By adventuring about, you become accustomed to the unexpected."

Amelia Earhart

arrived in New Guinea on June 29, 1937. They had flown 37,000 kilometres. The rest of their trip would be over the Pacific Ocean. On July 2, 1937, Earhart and Noonan took off. They were never seen again. Although the plane probably ran out of fuel and crashed in the sea, people still wonder about the duo's fate.

ABDICATION OF KING EDWARD VIII

▨ On December 11, 1936, King Edward VIII of Great Britain shocked the world. Edward wanted to marry American Wallis Simpson, but Simpson had been divorced. As king, Edward was the head of the Anglican Church, which did not approve of divorce. He had to choose between being king or marrying Simpson.

He announced that he would **abdicate** the throne to be with "the woman I love."

George VI became the next king. Three years later, he and Queen Elizabeth became the first British monarchs to visit Canada.

Spanish Civil War

The Spanish Civil War began in July 1936, when the army attempted to overthrow Spain's **democratic** government. General Francisco Franco led the army. He was supported by the Catholic Church, right-wing Spaniards, and by Italy's Mussolini and Germany's Hitler. These strong leaders provided troops, tanks, weapons, and

airplanes. The government received support from **Communists**, socialists, liberals, and from the Soviet Union. There were massacres on both sides.

In Canada, Catholics sent money to support Franco. Over 600 socialists and Communists volunteered to fight against

▨ Canadian soldiers formed several battalions to fight along side General Franco.

Franco. They formed the Mackenzie-Papineau Battalion, which was named after the two leaders of the 1837 rebellions in Canada. Canadian Prime Minister Mackenzie King did not want to anger Hitler and Mussolini. In 1937, he refused to allow any more volunteers to leave for Spain. The punishment for doing so was two years in prison.

The CCF was a strong political party. Party leaders met often to discuss how to get Canada and its economy back on track.

Radical Solutions to Hard Times

Something was wrong, and everyone knew it. There were no jobs and thousands of people were unemployed. Finding a solution was difficult. At every major street corner, members of different political parties tried to win support for their solutions. The solutions varied depending on who or what each party thought was to blame for causing the Great Depression.

The Co-operative Commonwealth Federation (CCF) party pointed a finger at the rich. They believed wealthy people kept all the money for themselves. The CCF wanted ordinary people, not wealthy individuals, to own banks and operate major industries. The CCF believed that a strong government could solve

Canada's economic problems. They thought that if people were educated about the issues, their knowledge would bring people around to the party's way of thinking.

Communists shared some ideas with the CCF. The Communist party thought that the only way to bring about change was through a violent **revolution**. They did not think education was enough to make a change.

Fascist parties, on the other hand, blamed the Depression on minority groups. They used people's fear of communism to attract more supporters. Their solution was to **deport** immigrants and appoint a strong leader much like Italy and Germany had.

1870–1947

Richard Bedford Bennett

Richard Bedford Bennett became leader of the Conservative party in 1927, and three years later he became the prime minister.

As prime minister, Bennett was a "one-man show." He did everything. According to one comedian, a meeting of the cabinet was Bennett talking to himself. But he worked extremely hard—up to eighteen hours a day. He dictated letters so fast that

two secretaries had trouble keeping up with him. The only day he took off was Sunday, because he had promised his mother that he would respect the **Sabbath**.

Prime Minister Bennett had promised to fight the Depression, but he could not do as he promised. People were frustrated and blamed him for the terrible economy. He lost the election in 1935.

On-To-Ottawa Trek

It began with the simple need to be heard. Many men were tired of the work camps. Some had been in the camps for almost three years. They wanted higher wages, more meaningful work, and freedom. In one British Columbia camp, 800 men decided to do something about their situation. Their idea was to ride to Ottawa on boxcars and present their demands to Prime Minister Bennett.

The trek began in Vancouver in the summer of 1935. As the men travelled east, they waved from the top of the boxcars to people along the way. Other unemployed men joined them. Everywhere, people yelled their support and provided food. One woman met the train with a bathtub filled with beef stew.

Unemployed Canadians felt that they had to do something. Many trekked to Ottawa to make their views known to the government.

By the time the men reached Regina, there were 1,800 aboard one hundred freight cars.

Then tragedy struck. Prime Minister Bennett thought the trek was a plot against his government. He ordered the RCMP to stop it in Regina.

The result was a riot on **Dominion Day**. When the RCMP attempted to arrest the trek's leaders, the men fought back with sticks, rocks, bottles, and bare hands. The riot lasted four hours. It left Regina in shambles. One policeman was accidently killed by the RCMP, and hundreds of people were injured. The police arrested 120 men for their part in the riot.

Adrian Arcand insisted that he and his newly founded National Unity Party would take over the country. His party fought communism and French Canadian nationalism.

Fascism and Nazism in Canada

Adrian Arcand was the leader of the Nazi Party in Quebec. As the Depression worsened, Arcand declared that the country needed a great leader. He blamed the growing unemployment on Communists and Jews.

Arcand formed the National Social Christian party in 1934. Members who could afford to paid a quarter each month. They wore blue shirts and trousers and put red and white swastika emblems on their shirt sleeves.

Each meeting began with the Lord's Prayer, the fascist salute, and pledges of loyalty to the king, Canada, and the party. By 1937, Arcand's fascist party had 700 card-carrying members.

When World War II began in 1939, Arcand planned to march to Ottawa and take over the country. Instead, Arcand and his supporters were arrested and sent to **internment** camps. Arcand called his internment camp, "Adolf Hitler Place" and renamed the two main streets "Goering" and "Goebbels"— after Hitler's top aides.

Getting Relief

In the 1930s, there was no employment insurance and no welfare payments. But the Depression created so many poor and unemployed people that the government had to help. To ensure that only people who "deserved" help received it, the government forced people to work for food. Some people were required to cut firewood and others pulled dandelions beside the road.

"I have seen men come into the office with tears in their eyes suffering humiliation at being forced to apply for assistance."

An Edmonton relief officer

Who got relief and who did not depended on the province, the town, and the person in charge. One relief officer refused to give a newly-married couple relief because he thought that people who married during such hard times should not expect any sympathy or help. If you applied for relief, you were not allowed to drink alcohol, own a phone, a radio, jewellery, or a car, or even have a driver's license. If you were seen drinking, driving a car, or at a race track, your relief was stopped.

Instead of money, people were given vouchers, which had to be spent in local stores. The people in charge of relief did not trust people not to drink or gamble

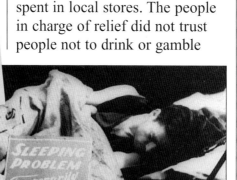

away money. There were no vouchers for soap, medicine, or cleaning supplies. Only the bare survival essentials were provided. For people forced to ask for help, it was a humiliating experience.

■ The Single Men's Unemployed Association marched in the streets. They wanted people to know that they wanted to work.

■ Many Canadians lived on the streets because they could not afford housing.

CONFLICT IN SCHOOLS

■ Jake Penner was a Communist politician. In 1932, he was elected alderman in Winnipeg. This caused some trouble in the community, as not everyone wanted Communists to have a role in the government. But Jake Penner was not the only one who felt the consequences of his election. Penner's position was held against his grade four son, Norman, in school.

"The wood-working instructor was a fascist....He used to beat me up regularly in the wood-working class. He would call me up to the front and before the whole class would say 'Well, Penner, I hear that they shot poor people in Russia for stealing some jam.' As soon as I opened my mouth to answer him he whacked me over the shoulder with a stick. He was a sadist. Everything I used to make he would break."

Norman Penner, whose father was a Communist

Riot at Christie Pits

Political tensions in the Canadian cities boiled over in the 1930s. In August 1933, a baseball game between a team of Italians and a team of Jews turned violent. The game had just finished. A Nazi group called the Pit Gang had shown up, waving a large flag with a swastika on it, chanting "Hail Hitler." Fighting began when the Jewish players and spectators tried to rip down the flag. Within minutes, both sides were waving axe handles, chains, lead pipes, and other weapons. People from the community came running to help their friends and family. The police were forced to swing their nightsticks to separate the Jews from the Pit Gang. Later, no one could even remember who had won the baseball game.

The trouble continued. Tensions increased as newspapers reported Hitler's persecution of German Jews. At one point, Toronto Jews were advised not to hold large gatherings to avoid any further confrontations.

Work Camps

By 1932, Prime Minister Bennett was worried. Canada had 70,000 homeless, unemployed young people. They were "roaming to and fro across the country," Bennett said, "particularly on freight trains, and are becoming a **menace** to the peace and even the safety of many communities along the railway." The prime minister was concerned that young people might become Communists and that they might try to overthrow the government. There had already been many hunger marches, strikes, and demonstrations.

■ People wanted meaningful work. Work camps gave work for the sake of work. It often made people more frustrated about the economy.

His solution was to create work camps for unemployed, single, young men. The camps were set up away from the cities. The men were sent to work at a variety of manual labour jobs in return for room and board, work clothes, and an allowance of 20 cents a day. Minimum wage at the time was around 50 cents an hour. Eventually, workers grumbled at the make-work projects they were forced to do. Some men were asked to dig a hole one day and then fill it the next.

Social Credit in Alberta

The Social Credit Party swept into power in Alberta in 1935. A record number of voters turned out to **oust** the United Farmers of Alberta party from office. This marked the first change in that government in fifteen years. The Social Credit, led by William Aberhart, came to office with little political experience. Aberhart was a respected school principal and a minister. But that was what the people wanted—Alberta would be led by everyday people like themselves. Voters welcomed Aberhart's ideas and looked forward to lower interest rates, full employment, and a better standard of living. Aberhart found it hard to deliver on his promises in office.

■ Aberhart was premier in 1935.

JUNE, 1938

ACTION COMICS

10¢

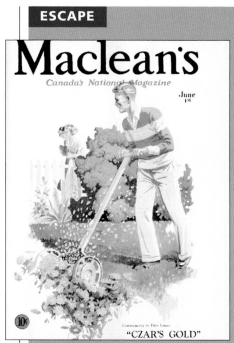

ESCAPE

Maclean's

Canada's National Magazine

June 1st

10¢

"CZAR'S GOLD"

Faster Than A Speeding Bullet

Superman was the brainchild of Jerry Siegel and Torontonian Joe Shuster in 1938. At first, Superman was a villain, but the two men decided he would make a better hero. The meek, mild-mannered reporter, Clark Kent, turned himself into a superhero when he heard the call of someone in trouble.

At first, the *Superman* comics were turned down by almost every comic publisher. Finally, Action Comics agreed to publish

Children read Superman faster than a speeding bullet. The Canadian-made hero dominated comic books for decades.

Superman. They thought that *Superman* was different enough to be successful.

Superman was an immediate success and inspired many other comic book producers to create their own "Superman" character. Superman was the first hero to have a secret identity and a special costume. In the first few books, Superman could leap tall buildings but could not fly. Over the years, Superman's powers increased to give readers bigger and bigger thrills.

People looked for ways to escape from hard times. Magazines provided one escape. Magazines such as *Maclean's*, *Liberty*, *Reader's Digest*, and *Life* provided romantic fictional stories that allowed readers to forget about their problems for a short while. Women's stories tended to focus on handsome, wealthy, strangers who carried the heroines away to strange, exotic places. The comings and goings of Hollywood stars also filled the pages of these monthly magazines.

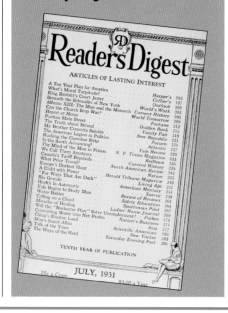

Reader's Digest

ARTICLES OF LASTING INTEREST

A Ten Year Plan for America
What's Moral Turpitude?
King Babbitt's Court Jester
Beneath the Sidewalks of New York
Alfonso XIII: The Man and the Monarch
Can the Church Stop War?
Heart at Home
Puritan Main Street
The Truth about Briand
My Brother Commits Suicide
The American Legion in Politics
Pushing the Cherokee Strip
Is this Youth Advancing?
The Mind of the Man in Prison
We Call Them Amateurs
Canada's Tariff Reprisals
What Price Travel?
Europe's Darkest Hour
A Child with Power
"For Ways That Are Dark"
Rio Grande
Health Is Automatic
Yale Begins to Study Man
Water Babies
Going on a Cloud
Miracles of Reading
Will the "Rochester Plan" Solve Unemployment?
Converting Waste into Net Profits
China's Shadow Land
Man's Insect Allies
Toll of the Town
The Ways of the Herd

Harper's 193
Collier's 197
Outlook 199
World's Work 202
Current History 206
World Tomorrow 209
Fortune 212
Golden Book 215
Vanity Fair 218
New Republic 221
Forum 224
Atlantic 227
Yale Review 230
N. Y. Times Magazine 233
Redbook 236
Current History 239
North American Review 242
Nation 245
Herald Tribune Magazine 248
Living Age 251
American Mercury 254
Survey 258
Review of Reviews 261
Safety Education 264
Sportsman Pilot 362
Ladies' Home Journal 269
Forbes 271
Nation's Business 274
Asia 277
Scientific American 280
New Yorker 283
Saturday Evening Post 286

TENTH YEAR OF PUBLICATION

JULY, 1931
25¢ a Copy $3.00 a Year

Canadian Writers Recognized with Award

In the 1930s, Canadian writers were recognized for their hard work and accomplishments. The Governor General's Literary Awards were first presented in 1937. They were created to highlight the great books written the previous year. The awards were presented by the Canadian Authors Association. This group chose the winners themselves until 1944. An independent board was then created to take over the selection of winners. The Governor General's Award remains one of the highest honours a Canadian author can receive in this country.

Gwethalyn Graham won the Governor General's Award for fiction in 1938. Bertram Brooker, Laura G. Salverson, and Franklin D. McDowell also won the award between 1936 and 1939.

Morley Callaghan

Morley Callaghan wrote about realistic topics. His books argued that people were in control of their own lives. If they failed, they only had themselves and their choices to blame. For material, he drew on the part-time jobs he held while a student and then as an employee with a daily newspaper in Toronto. They also gave him confidence that he could write well.

The 1930s was a productive period in Callaghan's career. He published seven volumes of fiction during this time, including *Such is My Beloved* and *More Joy in Heaven*. He also wrote scripts and journalism articles through the 1930s and 1940s.

Pulp Fiction

Inexpensive fiction novels were very popular. Because they were printed on cheap, brownish-paper, they were called pulp fiction—especially by people who did not approve of them. The covers often featured semi-nude women and the titles were sensational. The book titles included *Weird Tales*, *The Bride Wore Black*, *Listen to the Madman's Drum*, and *All These Must Die*.

These books made perfect reading for people who wanted to escape from their troubles. Canadian censors made sure that the more spicy covers and stories did not make it to Canadian book store shelves from the United States.

Critics did not think pulp fiction books were worthy literature. But Canadians could not get enough of them.

Epilepsy Treatment Discovered

In 1931, when Wilder Penfield stimulated a woman's brain with an **electrode**, she suddenly relived the experience of giving birth. Further experiments with other patients showed that in their subconscious, people remembered everything that they had heard and seen. They could be made to vividly recall these experiences by stimulating their brains with electrodes.

In 1933, Penfield used his discovery to help treat epilepsy. People with epilepsy suddenly, for no apparent reason, collapse and lose consciousness. When this happens, they are in danger of seriously injuring themselves.

With the patients wide-awake, Penfield stimulated their brains until they remembered the exact

Wilder Penfield's work with the brain influenced many surgeons across the world.

moment just prior to a seizure. Penfield then successfully destroyed the part of the brain that caused the seizure.

Easy-Off Oven Cleaner

Herbert McCool had a job fixing electric stoves and cleaning ovens. Cleaning ovens was a dirty, difficult task, and in 1933, McCool began to experiment with different chemicals to make his job easier. Caustic soda made the best cleaner, but it did not stick. When McCool discovered a method to make the soda stick to the oven walls, his job became much easier. It worked so well that McCool decided to market his new product, which he called Easy-Off.

The entire family helped. McCool's daughter Shirley designed the label by tracing a pattern from a perfume bottle. His wife, Doris, cooked and bottled the oven cleaner in the basement. Everyone took the bottles door to door, selling them for 50 cents each. When McCool died in 1946, the business was small, but profitable.

After McCool died, Doris gradually expanded the business. Later, she sold it to American Home Products. In 1984, Easy-Off was the highest-selling oven cleaner in Canada and the United States.

Home Conveniences at the End of the Decade

% Canadian Homes With:	Farm	All Canada
Electric Lights	20	69
Running Water	12	61
Telephones	29	40
Refrigerators	22	51
Indoor Flush Toilets	8	52

Norman Bethune, Chinese Hero

On his wedding day, Norman Bethune told his wife, "Now I can make your life a misery, but I'll never bore you." Bethune was never boring.

While working as a doctor in Montreal, Bethune became sympathetic to the problems of people living in poverty. When civil war erupted in Spain in 1936, Bethune **enlisted** to help the Spanish people keep their democratic government. On the battlefield, Bethune noticed that many wounded soldiers died from loss of blood on their way to the hospital. To solve this problem, Bethune organized a system for collecting blood, preserving it, and bringing it to the wounded for transfusions. His mobile blood clinics saved hundreds of lives.

In 1938, Bethune travelled to China to help fight the Japanese who had attacked China. He established a hospital to treat the wounded and to train doctors and nurses. When this hospital was destroyed by the Japanese, Bethune stayed close to the troops and performed operations near the fighting. Because there were only five qualified doctors, he worked eighteen-hour days. Tired and sick, Bethune began to think of home. "I sometimes dream of coffee, rare roast beef, of apple pie and ice cream.... Are books still being written? Is music still being played?" By the time Norman Bethune died in 1939, he had become a hero in China.

AUTOMOBILE DESIGN
The American automobile changed shape during the thirties. The Depression forced car makers to think of new ways to convince people to buy automobiles.

■ **North Americans rushed to get behind the wheel of a 1936 Ford.**

*At the beginning of the decade, cars were box-like in design. Most cars had wood-spoke wheels, solid tires, and foot boards. The car's body was mostly made of wood. To make them more attractive, automobiles were **streamlined** into a tear-drop shape. Cars now had rounded edges. The radiator grille was tilted back slightly to make the auto look faster. Low-pressure inner tube tires made driving more comfortable. A streamlined car also meant saving on fuel, which was important during the Depression. Another change was the use of chrome. To make the cars more attractive, radiator and wheel covers were chromed, and chrome strips were added to the body for ornamentation.*

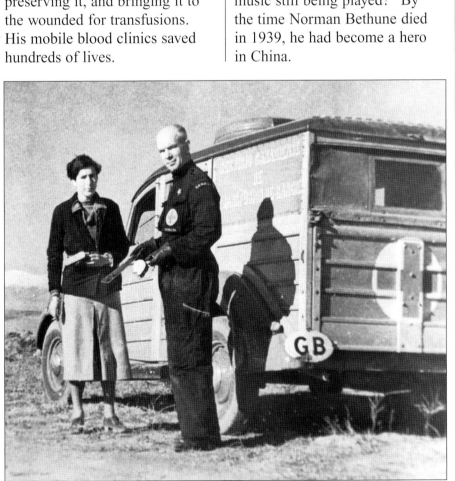

■ Norman Bethune drove his Canadian Blood Transfusion Unit across Spain to help the wounded during the Spanish Civil War.

Boxing Offers Escape

Boxing was popular in Canada. It ranked third in sports coverage behind only hockey and baseball. Some of Canada's boxers were also great performers. Jimmy McLarnin, for example, was a welterweight fighter who would do a forward somersault after knocking out his opponent. McLarnin was voted Canada's best boxer of the first half century.

Boxing offered young men an escape from slums. A preliminary bout paid $50 and even amateur boxers earned $5 a fight. Heavyweight champions earned more money than most famous baseball players and the best paid football coaches.

Boxers were often poor boys

Jimmy McLarnin, champion in 1934, was also referred to by his ethnicity. He was known as "the Vancouver Irishman."

who had been fighting for honour and survival on the street for most of their lives. Ethnic fighters created pride in their communities. Jewish boxers showed their toughness, contradicting stereotypes that Hitler and the Nazis spread through propaganda. Barney Ross, a Jewish boxer, said he felt as though he was fighting for all Jews. Many Jewish boxers wore the Star of David on their trunks. Promoters played on the ethnicity of the boxers—Ross was "the Hebrew Challenger," and when Max Baer fought Max Schmeling, the fight was called "Jew versus German."

WINNIPEG WINS CUP

In 1935, with only four Canadian-born players, Winnipeg captured the Grey Cup by defeating Hamilton 18-12. Western Canada had won its first Grey Cup game. "You should have been in Winnipeg that afternoon," a local magazine wrote. "Radios set out in the snowy streets blared of Winnipeg's triumph to shouting, cheering crowds. Moviegoers bellowed thunderously as the news was announced in theatres." The team was the "toast of the town."

However, the league was unhappy with the way Winnipeg had created such a powerful team. In February 1936, it ruled that no team could employ more than five non-Canadian players.

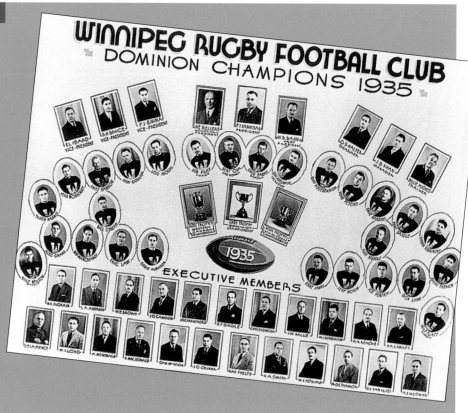

WINNIPEG RUGBY FOOTBALL CLUB
DOMINION CHAMPIONS 1935
EXECUTIVE MEMBERS

Eddie Shore

The best hockey showman was Eddie Shore of the Boston Bruins. Shore's rushes up the ice brought fans to their feet. Shore accumulated almost 1,000 stitches, fourteen broken noses, and five broken jaws during his career. In Boston he was a hero, while on the road he was a villain who often led the league in penalty minutes. Thanks to an adoring press, everyone knew that Shore liked to travel alone and only drank water in containers sent from Canada. In 1938, when the Bruins rejected his contract demands, Shore refused to play.

Eddie Shore was often called the "Iceman." He had a chilly style of hockey—he was emotionless and aggressive as he led the Bruins to the Stanley Cup.

Finally, with the fans chanting "We want Shore! We want Shore!" the team had to bring him back.

The start of a Boston game was pure entertainment. After both teams had warmed up, the lights were lowered and the crowd grew silent. Two ushers appeared at the entrance to the rink. One carried a talcum-powdered hockey stick; the other held the gate open for Shore. As Shore stepped on the ice, a spotlight illuminated him, the loudspeakers blasted out "Hail to the Chief," and the crowd broke into a deafening roar. Sporting a black and gold cape, and accompanied by a valet, Shore blew kisses to the fans as he slowly circled the rink.

Hockey Stars

The public eagerly followed the careers and personal lives of such sports personalities as Lionel Conacher, Syl Apps, Frank Boucher, Joe Primeau, Francis "King" Clancy, and Ivan Johnson. Aurel Joliat, the idol of French Canada, usually wore a black baseball cap when he played. "King" Clancy, a 147-pound, hard-hitting hockey defenseman with a fiery temper, could whip crowds into a frenzy.

Howie Morenz was nicknamed "the human projectile" for his habit of throwing up his arms and spinning into a spreadeagle collapse on the ice in an attempt to draw a penalty on an opposing player. His reckless style and headlong rushes up the ice earned him a reputation as the Babe Ruth of hockey. When Morenz died in 1937 from a blood clot as a result of crashing into the boards, 200,000 people lined the parade route to the cemetery in Quebec.

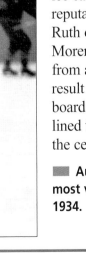

Aurel Joliat was the most valuable player in 1934.

End of the Montreal Hockey Rivalry

Ada Mackenzie

Ada Mackenzie was Canada's best female golfer. She won the Canadian Ladies' Amateur Open in 1919, 1925, 1926, 1933 and 1935. Later, she captured the Canadian Women's Senior Golf Championship eight times.

Mackenzie was an **innovator** in women's golf clothing and established Ada Mackenzie Ltd., a successful women's clothing store in Toronto. While playing in the U.S. Women's Amateur Championship, she decided that her clothing was not suitable for golfing. "I was wearing wool, my sleeves were down over my wrists and the skirt was sloughing in the mud. It was just the completely wrong outfit. I lost the match but it was that experience that got me into the ladies' sportswear business."

The Montreal Maroons helped create an exciting rivalry within Quebec.

The Montreal Maroons catered to the English Canadians in Montreal and enjoyed a natural rivalry with the French-favoured Montreal Canadiens. However, when the two Montreal teams traded players, the illusion of bitter rivalry became hard to maintain and attendance at the games fell. The Maroons pleaded for assistance, but the NHL refused to help. The Maroons collapsed in 1938, just three years after winning the Stanley Cup.

THE BUSINESS OF GOLF

The cost of golf clothing, green fees, equipment, and caddies limited the number of people who played golf during the Depression. Most people thought golf was a gentleman's game. The game was popular among businessmen, who closed business deals as they played and later socialized in the clubhouse.

Although golf was fashionable in every province, it was more popular in large, urban areas. The Alberta Golf Association promoted golf in rural areas by arranging tours of top golfers. It also allowed members of small town golf clubs to play at urban clubs. Ontario and Quebec dominated Canada's golfing scene.

More women golfed in the 1930s than previous decades. There were no professional tournaments for women. Golfer Marjorie Kirkham of Montreal was an exception to the rule. She captured the 1930 Canadian amateur title, and the following year she reached the finals of both the Canadian open, which anyone could compete in, and the closed, in which a player needed an invitation. In 1932 she won the Canadian Ladies' Open championships. She then became the first female teaching pro in North America.

Lady Bessborough Trophy

Many women played hockey in the 1930s. Although the Canadian Intercollegiate Women's Ice Hockey League collapsed in 1933, women's teams from every region of Canada challenged for the Lady Bessborough Trophy that was donated in 1935 for the national championship. Female leagues included teams of factory workers, department store clerks, telephone company operators, and secretaries.

Outstanding teams included the Red Deer Amazons, the Edmonton Rustlers, the Montreal Maroons, and the Summerside (Prince Edward Island) Crystal Sisters. The Preston Rivulettes won 348 of 350 games during the decade and captured the Lady Bessborough Trophy six times.

■ The Preston Rivulettes were a hockey dynasty in the thirties.

Hockey Violence

In 1934, Toronto Maple Leaf "Ace" Bailey's hockey career, and almost his life, was ended when an Eddie Shore body check cracked his skull. The incident took place at the Boston Gardens on December 12, 1933. Late in the game, "King" Clancy checked Eddie Shore against the boards in the Boston end. Shore thought that Bailey had checked him. Skating down the ice at full speed, Shore spotted Bailey resting on his hockey stick. Approaching Bailey from behind, Shore hit him in the kidneys with his right shoulder. Bailey somersaulted backwards and hit his head on the ice.

Seeing his teammate injured, Red Horner skated up to Shore and punched him in the jaw. According to one witness, Shore's head hit the ice, "splitting open. In an instant, he was circled by a pool of blood about three feet in diameter."

By now the crowd was in an uproar. Police had to

> "We heard a crack you might compare to the sound of smashing a pumpkin with a baseball bat. Bailey was lying on the blue line with his head turned sideways, as though his neck were broken. His knees were raised, legs twitching."
>
> Frank Selke,
> Toronto Maple Leaf
> Assistant Manager

restrain the fans as the Leafs retired to their dressing room.

Newspapers carried daily bulletins as Bailey had two operations for his fractured skull. Toronto fans called Shore an animal, and demanded that he be banned from hockey for life. Bailey's father bought a gun and took the train to Boston, where he intended to even the score. Bailey recovered, but his career was over.

■ There were no hard feelings as Ace Bailey and Eddie Shore shook hands after their scuffle.

Rotten Potatoes, Rotten Tomatoes

During the Great Depression, Canadians had too much of everything except money and jobs. In Prince Edward Island, potatoes were left to rot in the soil because no one could afford to buy them. The same was true of tomatoes in British Columbia. The problem was that because of their financial problems, farmers could not buy such items as farm equipment, seeds, fertilizer, and clothes. The stores that usually sold these goods were left with full shelves. Stores stopped ordering goods from manufacturers. With fewer orders, manufacturers laid off workers. These workers could no longer afford to buy things. This led to more lay-offs. People stopped believing that things would get better.

People drove older cars and stopped going to doctors and dentists to save money. They wore patched clothes. Children went barefoot in the summer and saved their socks to use as gloves in the winter. Flour sacks made good underwear, and cardboard filled holes in shoes. People saved money any way they could.

■ Times were tough across Canada. People were starving, yet food was rotting because there was no one to buy it.

A Stinky Bargain

Before the depression, a Maritime company had tried to raise skunks for their pelts. When the public showed no interest in skunk fur, the forty animals were set free. Soon, Prince Edward Island was overrun with skunks. The government offered 50 cents per skunk snout. This was one way to earn money during the Depression. Some people even went to Nova Scotia to illegally trap skunks. One imaginative person made fake snouts from cow hide. In three years, the government paid bounties on over 15,000 skunks.

Depression Prices

Prices dropped during the Depression. Farmers could not make any money selling their goods.

	Before	During
Wheat	$1.63	$1.35
Dozen eggs	$0.30	$0.08
Silver fox pelt	$100.00	$28.00
Pork	$0.16	$0.03
100 pounds of potatoes	$1.50	$0.06

On Strike

In 1936, workers at the Kelsey Wheel Company in Windsor, Ontario, decided they had had enough. They took part in Canada's first sit-down strike against low wages, long hours, and dangerous working conditions. This meant workers sat at their machines and would not work or leave. While not a total success, they won some of their demands.

The Hard Numbers

Average Yearly Income Per Person

	1928	1933
British Columbia	$590	$310
Alberta	$550	$210
Saskatchewan	$480	$140
Manitoba	$470	$240
Ontario	$550	$310
New Brunswick	$290	$180
Nova Scotia	$320	$210
PEI	$280	$150
Canada	$470	$250

Such tactics were not always successful. A Sarnia, Ontario, company sent in men to beat strikers with baseball bats. Police and the government took the company's side and would not protect the strikers.

In 1937, there were 278 strikes in 125 communities. One of the most significant strikes took place at General Motors in Oshawa, Ontario. Although General Motors had increased its profits the previous year, it cut wages for the fifth time in five years. Workers walked off the job in protest. They demanded the right to join a union and have the union negotiate better wages on their behalf. They also wanted a rest period, a regular work week, and time and a half wages for overtime work. The company refused these demands at first. However, it began to fear that other companies would take much of its business if the strike lasted too long. After 15 days, the company gave in and the workers returned to their jobs.

■ Strikes took other forms. Unemployed workers used hunger strikes to make the government truly realize the problems.

Working Conditions

Since so many people were unemployed, companies were able to force their employees to work long hours for low wages. When factories were busy, employees worked over 60 hours a week, including Saturday. There was no overtime pay. As one worker noted, "you were like firemen—you were always on call."

Jobs were difficult to obtain. When an Edmonton store advertised for salesgirls, the next day hundreds of women formed a line that circled the entire block. Since the store only had three positions available, there was a riot.

Some companies made a fortune. They paid their employees very little and charged high prices for their goods. A government commission found, for example, that while Eaton's paid seamstresses 9.5 cents for sewing a dozen dresses, each dress was sold for $1.59.

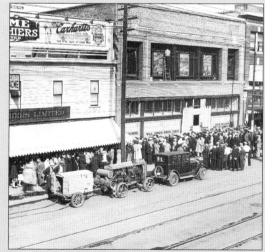

■ Hundreds of people lined up for six job openings at the Army & Navy store in Regina.

The Best Dressed Sporting Man

The thirties man had many looks. The sporty gentleman had different outfits for different sports.

For golf he wore tweed knickerbockers, which were loose pants gathered at the knee or calf, and heavy stockings. Over this he wore silk or flannel shirts and a woolen jacket. Younger men wore short pants called *plus fours* for golf and other casual occasions.

For tennis, the style was a white flannel coat with long trousers. Sometimes, if it was hot, he wore a fine white sweater instead of a coat.

On boating trips, the thirties man wore long white cotton or linen trousers and a navy blue coat. To finish off the look, he wore a peaked yachting cap.

When it was time for a dip in the pool, the thirties man had to follow the rules at the beach. On some beaches, it was still illegal for a man to be topless in public.

■ Short pants were the rage for men on the golf course.

A BUSINESSMAN'S APPEARANCE

■ He should have a bath everyday.
■ He should use a toothbrush several times a day.
■ He should keep his fingernails clean and his hair well brushed.
■ His shoes should be polished.
■ His hair at the back should be layered.
■ His clothes must be conservative in style and quiet in colour.
■ His trousers should be creased properly.
■ If he plans to remove his coat, he must wear a belt rather than suspenders.
■ Jackets should have wide, peaked lapels and trousers should be pleated in the front.

Hosiery a Fashion Craze

Nylon was discovered in 1937. It was used to make parachutes and, more importantly to women at the end of the Depression, Nylon stockings. Women could wear Nylon stockings under their dresses everyday. The stockings were fairly expensive, at $1.15 a pair, but they were worth the money. These artificial stockings lasted longer than silk and could stand up to more wear-and-tear. For the budget-conscious woman, Nylon stockings were often the only option.

Women's Fashions

Fashions are always changing. In the 1920s, the "boyish look" was the rage. The waist in women's clothing disappeared. Bustlines were flat, and the hemline was just above the knee. Clothing was loose-fitting and hung straight down from the shoulders. This changed in the 1930s. The waist returned, and the flat silhouette was gone. Skirts clung to the figure and hemlines dropped to mid-calf.

By 1933, padded shoulders, fitted sleeves, narrow waists, and high necklines were "in." Fashionable women wore "nude" shades of stockings, high spiked heels, large hats with flowers and bows, nail polish, and gloves. At the end of the decade, necklines were lower, hemlines began to rise again, and brighter colours became popular. Influenced by movie stars, younger women began wearing slacks. Bathing suits, however, were still required to have short skirts attached.

■ Fashion was varied in the 1930s. Some women dressed in the latest fashions, while others (above right) preferred the practicality of pants.

■ Boys' and girls' fashions were short—short pants and short skirts were a must for children.

"For a girl up to eight years of age, who has well formed legs, skirts should be quite short, some distance above the knees. When a girl reaches eight or nine years, her skirts come down closer to the knees. Socks are appropriate up to twelve years of age. Jewels are not worn by little girls, except for a string of pearls, a slender gold chain with a pendant, and a few simple brooches. Boys' clothing is equally simple. The two-piece Jersey suits in fine wool are nice for boys from two to five years. Sailor suits, having long or knee length blue serge trousers, and white or blue silk blouses, with sailor collars, are popular for lads up to ten or twelve years."

Gertrude Pringle
in *Etiquette in Canada*

Anti-Jewish Feelings in in Canada

During hard times, prejudice against different ethnic groups often increased. In the 1930s, Canadian Jews often faced **discrimination**. Signs on store fronts declared "No Jews wanted" or "No Jews or dogs allowed." Jews were refused admission to clubs. Insurance companies either refused to insure them or charged higher rates. Whole suburbs were closed to Jewish families. The courts upheld landlords' rights to not sell houses to Jewish buyers.

Jewish people were judged more by their ethnicity than by their personalities or abilities. McGill University in Montreal required Jews to have higher grades than other students to be accepted. The staff of a

Jewish Hunger Marchers protested the unfair treatment of Jewish people in Canada.

Montreal hospital refused to care for Jewish patients. The list of injustices went on and on during the 1930s and 1940s.

S.S. St. Louis Turned Away

In the spring of 1939, the *S.S. St. Louis* set sail with 930 Jewish passengers. These people had escaped from Germany, where Hitler had begun a program to take away all their freedoms. Cuba and the United States refused to allow the ship to port. The Americans even had the *St. Louis* followed to make sure no one swam to shore.

In Canada, there was some support and compassion for these **exiles**, but most Canadians were not sympathetic. Policymakers would not give in to pressure to allow these people to stay as refugees. Eventually, Prime Minister Mackenzie King refused to allow the ship to dock in Canada. The passengers had to return to Europe and Hitler's rule.

The government would not allow the Jewish would-be immigrants to stay in Canada.

DEPORTATION

In 1930, the government passed a law to stop almost all immigration to Canada. Only those people with a considerable amount of money were allowed to immigrate. With so few jobs available, most Canadians agreed with the new law.

Some recent immigrants experienced a great deal of discrimination. Others were deported and sent back to the country from which they had come. According to the law, immigrants who could not support themselves could be deported. Many cities took advantage of this law to deport people rather than provide them with support. Some employers used the law to have union organizers deported. Between 1930 and 1935, about 30,000 immigrants were deported.

People, including many Scandinavian immigrants, saw Canada as a new start.

Depressed Immigration

During the Great Depression, very few people could break through the government's restrictions and immigrate to Canada. Only members of the immediate family of people already living in Canada were permitted to enter the country. Farmers who had the money to start a farm were also allowed to immigrate.

These policy restrictions greatly affected the number of immigrants becoming Canadian citizens. In the 1920s, more than one million people entered Canada's borders from other countries. In the 1930s there was only around 250,000.

Immigrants to Canada

Year	Number
1930	104,810
1931	27,530
1932	20,530
1933	14,380
1934	12,480
1935	11,280
1936	11,640
1937	15,100
1938	17,240
1939	16,990

Popular Music

The 1930s were known as the "swing era" and the "big band era." One of the best-known musicians was Louis Armstrong. He made music called swing popular. As the name suggests, this music had a lively, upbeat rhythm that lifted people's spirits.

This sound was soon adopted by the big bands of Count Basie, Tommy Dorsey, Benny Goodman, and Guy Lombardo's Royal Canadians. Big bands got their name from the large group of instruments they used—including saxophones, trombones, trumpets, clarinets, and a rhythm section of piano, bass, drums, and guitar. The big bands played dance music and featured vocalists, such as Frank Sinatra and Connie Boswell, who enchanted audiences with their romantic lyrics.

Most of the songs Canadians listened to came from the United States. Famous American big bands played to packed houses in Canada. Everywhere, groups of young people across Canada scraped together enough money to form their own bands and move from town to town in "one-night stands."

The music of Tommy Dorsey and his band kept Canadians humming along through the 1930s.

Guy Lombardo's Big Band

Guy Lombardo started his career playing **gigs** at school with his seven brothers. In 1919, he formed the Lombardo Royal Canadian Orchestra, which became the longest-running act in show business history. The group made more hit songs than any other musical organization. The Lombardo New Year's Eve Party, which began in 1929, was the longest-running annual special program in radio history.

Lombardo worked hard to make his audience enjoy the music. People said that if you could move your legs at all, you could dance to his music. Many of the bands' songs were famous—"Seems Like Old Times," "Boo Hoo," "Sweethearts on Parade," and "Bye Bye Blues" were chart-toppers. Guy Lombardo was remembered for his easy music style up until his death in 1977.

Guy Lombardo (second from right) played music with his brothers at the start of his career. He went on to become a Canadian music legend.

Welcoming the Blues

During the 1930s, the blues became a national craze. Records by blues singers including Bessie Smith, filled stores and people's homes by the millions. The blues spread northward with the migration of many African Americans in the southern United States. Their music began to enter the shows of big band and jazz musicians in both Canada and the United States.

Blues lyrics were often very personal. People could relate well to the words in the song. They frequently dealt with the pain of love and betrayal. Blues musicians sang about unhappy situations that many people shared— being jobless during the Depression, being hungry, broke, and far from home and families.

■ Bessie Smith's blues songs hit close to home for many Canadians.

FOLK ROOTS

■ Woody Guthrie was one of the leaders of the folk music era. He took any topic and quickly wrote a melody with lyrics. His songs included the "Dust Bowl Refugees" and "Dust Pneumonia Blues," which discussed the great dust storm on the prairies. Guthrie once said, "A folk song is what's wrong and how to fix it, or who's out of work and where the job is, or who's broke and where the money is."

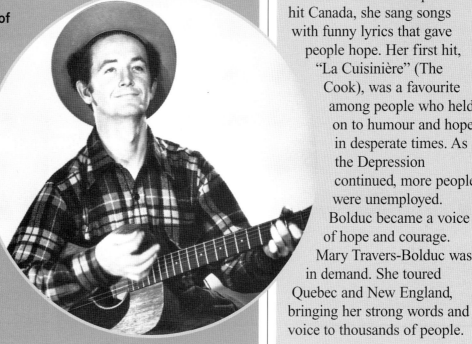

Singer Gives Hope

French-Canadian entertainer Mary Travers-Bolduc made the Great Depression a little more bearable for Canadians. She made them laugh during hard times with her witty songs. She sang about everyday life for everyday Canadians in the 1930s. She sang songs about the Dionne Quintuplets and World War II—songs people could relate to and understand.

Bolduc's singing career began in music festivals with friends. People were impressed by her talent and the spirit that shone through when she sang and played the fiddle. By the end of the 1920s, she was writing her own songs and was offered a contract for five albums.

When the Great Depression hit Canada, she sang songs with funny lyrics that gave people hope. Her first hit, "La Cuisinière" (The Cook), was a favourite among people who held on to humour and hope in desperate times. As the Depression continued, more people were unemployed. Bolduc became a voice of hope and courage. Mary Travers-Bolduc was in demand. She toured Quebec and New England, bringing her strong words and voice to thousands of people.

Dionne Quintuplets Capture Hearts

Elzire Dionne had already given birth to two tiny baby girls. When Dr. Allan Dafoe arrived at the Dionne farmhouse on May 28, 1934, a third baby was on its way. Then, another. And another. In the end there were five identical baby girls—quintuplets.

Elzire was 25 years old. She had been married to Oliva for nine years. They already had five children. When Oliva heard the news he collapsed. For days he had trouble sleeping, he was so worried about how he was going to feed so many children.

The babies—Annette, Cecile, Emilie, Marie, and Yvonne— quickly became front page news around the world. When papers reported that Oliva was going to show the girls at the Chicago

Canadians from coast to coast watched the Dionne quintuplets grow up.

World's Fair for $50,000, the Ontario government took the babies away from their parents. The government was worried that the girls would be harmed by going to the fair.

The government hired an expert in child care to raise the children. The girls became Canada's biggest tourist attraction. More people visited the quints than Niagara Falls— over 6,000 people a day. Tourists could watch the girls from behind one-way glass walls from eleven in the morning to three in the afternoon. These girls were the best known infants in the world. They were not reunited with their parents until 1943.

Women and Work

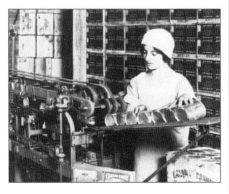

Women, many people believed at this time, were not serious about their work, did not make good workers, and took jobs away from men who needed to work to support their families. In many places, women were expected to resign as soon as they married. To keep their jobs, some women had lengthy engagements, or married in secret.

RAISING CHILDREN

How should children be raised? In the 1930s, "the experts" decided that raising a child was like running a factory. Everything that children did should be done on to a schedule. Mothers were told that feeding, bedtimes, exercise and bowel movements should be as regular as clockwork. Babies should cry for a few moments each day to expand their lungs, but if the mother came every time the child cried, the baby would grow up to be selfish.
Experts said that too much cuddling and kissing was harmful, and frequent handling could cause spinal curvature, bone deformities, irritability, and slowed growth.

Bennett Buggies

With no money to buy gasoline to operate their tractors and other farm machinery, western farmers turned to their horses. Since their cars were useless without gasoline, farmers took out the engine, removed the windshields, and attached their automobile to a team of horses. The new "cars" were called Bennett Buggies after the prime minister.

Rich and Poor in Canada

There was a large difference between the classes in the 1930s. There were many people who could not feed themselves and their families. There was also a number of Canadians with incredible wealth. A part of the population was essentially untouched by the Depression. They continued to dress in tuxedos and entertain friends with elaborate parties.

■ Those in high society had to follow many rules. They had to know how to dress, when to shake hands, and when to bow. Other Canadians worried about how they would find food to eat.

Making Ends Meet

Housing was a problem. Unable to afford rent, many families shared their homes. To "make ends meet," families often took in lodgers. As one housewife in Flin Flon, Manitoba, stated, "It just means having an extra mouth to feed, I'd throw a few more dumplings in the pot, wash some extra clothes, make another bed. What's one more to care for when you're already doing work?"

HOBOES

■ Called hoboes, tramps, or knights of the road, approximately 300,000 young men left home during the Depression to look for work. Jumping aboard freight trains, they criss-crossed the country. One hobo, Francis Furlotte, crossed Canada eight times.

Tramps usually slept in what were called hobo "jungles" near major railway junctions. These were areas where unemployed or homeless people gathered near towns and cities. From here, they went into the city to beg for food. They returned at night with whatever food they had been given, which was cooked by the hobo chef. Most other hoboes ate their meals at soup kitchens in town. Churches and charities offered free food to hoboes and the poor at these soup kitchens.

It was easy to spot a hobo. He was unshaven and needed a haircut. He wore dirty, ragged clothing. He often carried small tin cans for people to put money in.

American Influence in Sports

Hard times resulted in the National Hockey League (NHL) becoming more American. Some teams **folded** and other clubs moved to larger cities. Following the collapse of the Montreal Maroons, a sports writer wrote, "[I hope] that the National Hockey League will build for the future to assure that Canadian teams will continue in what is the major domain of our great winter pastime."

There were similar problems in football. The name "rugby" was replaced by "rugby football" and "touchdown" was now used instead of the word "try." It was a pity, some people said, "to see us imitate Americans." Sports writer Leslie Roberts protested that Canadians were "taking our cues from our cousins beyond the border, reconstructing our major games to appeal to the watcher rather than the players—because these games have become specialized branches of Big Business."

The Toronto Maple Leafs managed to stay alive during the Americanization of the NHL. They won their first Stanley Cup championship in 1932.

Owning the Radio Waves

At night, it was easier for most people in Alberta to listen to an American radio station, or even one from Mexico, than a Canadian broadcast. There were two problems. Two or more radio stations could broadcast on the same radio wave. Neither came through really clearly because they interfered with each other. An agreement between Canada and the United States in 1937 gave Canada six frequencies and the countries shared twenty-four others. The United States got the remaining ninety-four frequencies. Most American stations were at least twenty times more powerful than Canadian stations. In some rural areas of the province, 40 percent of the population could not get a Canadian station that did not have a lot of static.

Whereas most privately owned stations relied on American programming, by law the CBC had to offer mostly Canadian content. In 1938, for example, the CBC had sixty and a half hours of Canadian programs, twenty-six hours of American, and twelve hours of overseas programs.

TRADE

It was a long time coming, and the trade deal caused a great deal of dispute between the representatives of the two countries during the late 1930s. Prime Minister Mackenzie King and United States President Franklin Roosevelt finally signed the trade agreement. The treaty was intended to make trade across the border easier. It allowed Canadian farmers, lumber sellers, and fishermen to make more money from American sales. The import and export taxes were reduced. It would now cost Canadians less money to sell in the American market.

The "Great Woods"

PRIMITIVE PASSIONS! GRIPPING STORY OF LOVE AND VENGEANCE IN THE CANADIAN WILDS!

BATTLES FOR LOVE IN THE WILD SETTING OF THE GREAT NORTH LAND!

The above were typical Hollywood advertisements for movies supposedly filmed in Canada. In Hollywood's eyes, Canada was a snowswept "Great Woods." Movies with Canadian themes including *Men of the North, Mounted Fury, Klondike, Sign of the Wolf,* and *On the Great White Trail* flooded movie theatres.

Why did Hollywood set so many of its films in Canada? To many Americans, Canada sounded exotic—wild and **primitive**, slightly dangerous, and scenic. Canadians were shown as simple, unsophisticated people. Moviegoers flocked to exciting, romantic films about the "Great Woods of the North." The films were about Canada and Canadian themes, but the majority of these movies were filmed in the United States. Regardless, Hollywood

■ Mounties were popular characters in Hollywood during the 1920s and 1930s.

had discovered a winning and profitable formula that movie producers used again and again.

About half of the movies made about Canada featured a Mountie (or Mounties) in the plot. Hollywood's Mountie character was courteous, kind, brave, trustworthy, and almost always got his man. He usually got his girl, too!

Canadian and American Trade Relations Improve

In 1930, Canada and the United States began a **tariff** war. The Americans passed the Hawley-Smoot Tariff, which increased the duty paid on imports. Tariffs reached the highest levels in history. Canada reacted by raising its own tariffs. Prime Minister Bennett promised Canadians that he would charge into international markets and decrease Canada's dependence on the United States. In 1932, Bennett hosted

the Imperial Economic Conference in Ottawa. It worked to encourage trade and change the tariff system within the British Commonwealth.

By 1934, trade between the two countries began to improve. After the United States

passed the Reciprocal Trade Agreements, the two governments met to figure out the best way to lower tariffs and increase trade. In 1935, Prime Minister King finished off the trade agreement started by Bennett. A second and more far-reaching agreement was entered into in 1938. This led to tariffs between Canada and the United States being reduced even further. This cooperation and acceptable trade relations helped both countries during the onset of World War II.

Where did it happen?

Match each number with an event.

a) Where the Dionne quintuplets were born

b) Where the On-To-Ottawa Trek was stopped

c) Home of the first Western team to win the Grey Cup

d) Mary Travers-Bolduc's home province

e) Mine disaster at Moose River

f) Site where On-To-Ottawa trek began

g) Province with too many skunks

h) Where the Stork Derby took place

Trivia Challenge

1. During the 1930s, the number of immigrants to Canada

a) increased
b) stayed the same
c) decreased

2. Norman Bethune became a hero in

a) Russia, Germany
b) China, Spain
c) Canada, Mexico

3. Percentage of Canadian homes with in-door flush toilets in 1939

a) 95
b) 82
c) 52

4. The Dionne Quintuplets were

a) a jazz group
b) a group of artists
c) five babies

5. Canada's prime ministers during most of the 1930s was

a) Bennett
b) King
c) Mulroney

Answers: 1. c; 2. b;
3. c; 4. c; 5. a.

Newsmakers

Match the name in the news with their role in the 1930s!

a) hockey player

b) Canadian prime minister

c) boxer

d) big band leader

e) mobile blood transfusions

f) leader of Germany

g) invented Superman

h) leader of Canadian Fascist Party

i) America's Sweetheart

j) hockey broadcaster

1. R.B. Bennett
2. Adrian Arcand
3. Adolf Hitler
4. Norman Bethune
5. Jimmy McLarin
6. Mary Pickford
7. Foster Hewitt
8. Joe Shuster
9. Eddie Shore
10. Guy Lombardo

Answers: 1. b; 2. h; 3. f; 4. e;
5. c; 6. i; 7. j; 8. g; 9. a; 10. d.

abdicate: to give up

bankrupt: broke and unable to pay off debts

boycotted: refused, as a group, to support a person or business

Communist: a political system in which the state controls all property and methods of production

democratic: a system in which the citizens elect officials to represent their wishes

deport: send back to one's country of origin

dictatorship: when people claim the government without the support of the people or any inherited right to it

discrimination: treating a person or group differently based on assumptions about their race, religion, or lifestyle

drought: a long period of dry weather

Dominion Day: holiday celebrating the establishment of the dominion of Canada, July 1, 1867; it is now called Canada Day

electrode: a place where an electric current flows into or out of a device

enlisted: joined the army

exiles: people who were sent away from their countries as punishment

folded: stopped operating

gigs: an engagement for a band or singer

inferior: lower in position or rank

innovator: someone who starts something new

internment: forcing people to stay in one area for political reasons, usually during a war

jockey club: place to bet on horse racing

menace: a threat

mustard gas: a poison that causes burns, blindness, and death; often used as a weapon in war

oust: to force out

primitive: having to do with an early or first stage of development

propaganda: ideas that are spread to try to influence other people's way of thinking

realism: art that pictures nature accurately

revolution: using force to overthrow the government and set up another one

Sabbath: often Sunday, the day set aside for worship

sadist: person who draws pleasure from cruelty to another person

secluded: far away from

shrill: having a sharp, high sound

streamlined: a shape designed to offer as little resistance as possible for motion through air or water

swastika: a symbol of a cross with arms of equal length bent at right angles; Nazi Germany adopted the symbol to represent their beliefs

tariff: a charge or tax that a government puts on goods coming into the country

Learning More

Here are some book resources and Internet links if you want to learn more about the people, places, and events that made headlines during the 1930s.

Books

Brown, Craig. *The Illustrated History of Canada*. Toronto: Lester & Orpen Dennys, 1987.

Deir, Elspeth. *Canada: Years of Change*. Ontario: Holt, Rinehart and Winston of Canada, 1982.

Routh, Caroline. *In Style: 100 Years of Canadian Women's Fashion*. Toronto: Stoddart Publishing, 1993.

Twentieth Century Canada. Calgary, Alberta: Weigl Educational Publishers, 1996.

The Junior Encyclopedia of Canada. Edmonton: Hurtig Publishers, 1990.

Internet Links

There are many sites on the internet that will help you learn more about the 1930s. Here are a few to explore.

http://www.heritage.excite.sfu.ca/pmg/depress/greatdepress.html
This site provides information about Canada during the Great Depression.

http://www.macabees.ab.ca/canada
This site offers Canadian information on various topics. It is a great site for historical data as well as current Canadian information.

http://Home.InfoRamp.Net/~cshof
For people who love sports, this provides information about athletes inducted into the Canadian Sports Hall of Fame, including biographies and photographs.

Some web sites stay active longer than others. To find more information about Canada during this decade, use an Internet search engine. Your search words may include "Canada and the 1930s" or "Canada and the Great Depression." You may also want to enter specific names you read about in this book to find out more.